BoomWhack Attack!

Music Fun With Boomwhackers® and Other Instruments

Arranged by Tom Anderson

MW00816502

Table of Contents

PLAYBACK+
Speed • Pitch • Balance • Loop

DIGITAL DOWNLOAD CODE
To access AUDIO MP3s, go to:
www.halleonard.com/mylibrary

Enter Code
1231-3286-6858-3722

ISBN: 978-1-4234-2419-2

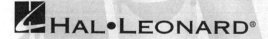

Copyright © 2007 by HAL LEONARD CORPORATION
International Copyright Secured   All Rights Reserved

Visit Hal Leonard Online at
www.halleonard.com

Contact Us:
Hal Leonard
7777 West Bluemound Road
Milwaukee, WI 53213
Email: info@halleonard.com

In Europe contact:
Hal Leonard Europe Limited
Distribution Centre, Newmarket Road
Bury St Edmunds, Suffolk, IP33 3YB
Email: info@halleonardeurope.com

In Australia contact:
Hal Leonard Australia Pty. Ltd.
4 Lentara Court
Cheltenham, Victoria, 3192 Australia
Email: info@halleonard.com.au

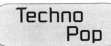

BoomWhack Attack!

Audio
Access

VOCALS

BOOMWHACKERS – Notes Used: D, F, G, A, B, C'

Words and Music by
TOM ANDERSON

C.C. Rider

Audio
Access

BOOMWHACKERS – Notes Used: C, D, E, F, G, A, B, C'

Traditional
Arranged by TOM ANDERSON

* Pitched instruments

Set up instruments with these pitches. Improvise a solo
with these notes the 3rd time through the song (meas. 29).

Copyright © 2005 by HAL LEONARD CORPORATION
International Copyright Secured   All Rights Reserved

BoomWhack Attack!

Blues

C.C. Rider

Audio Access

VOCALS

Traditional
Arranged by TOM ANDERSON

BoomWhack Attack!

29 G13

29   Vibes solo using these pitches: G B♭ C D F G

C9   G13

33

D9   C9   G13   **D.S. al Coda**

37

CODA

You made me love you, now your friend has come.

G7   D9   C7

41

N.C.   G13   *fills*

44

Jamaica Farewell

BOOMWHACKERS – Notes Used: C, D, E, F, G, A, B, C'

Traditional Caribbean
Arranged by TOM ANDERSON

PERCUSSION INSTRUMENTS *(repeat patterns throughout)*

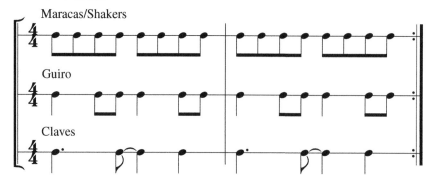

BoomWhack Attack!

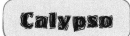

Jamaica Farewell

Traditional Caribbean
Arranged by TOM ANDERSON

Audio Access

VOCALS

1. In Ja - mai - ca, where hearts are light,___ where the mu - sic has___ you danc - ing all the night,___ a boy was walk - ing a - long the pier,___ he sang a lit - tle song___ that I still can hear.___ } Oh, so

2. In Ja - mai - ca, you play and fish,___ and the Yan - kee dol - lar buys you what you wish.___ I was so hap - py with ev - 'ry - thing,___ and yet it made me sad___ when I heard him sing:___ }

sad am I___ to say, "Good - bye."___ I'll come back,___ no more will I cry,___ I

(3rd time)
To Coda ⊕

Dm

hate   to   say,___   "Fare - well,   Ja - mai - ca"   to - day,___   be - cause   the

C/G   G7 | 1 Dm/G   C   *(to beginning)* | 2 Dm/G   C   **D.S. al Coda**

place   I   love   is   here,   down   King - ston   Way!_   King - ston   Way!_   Oh,   so

⊕ **CODA**

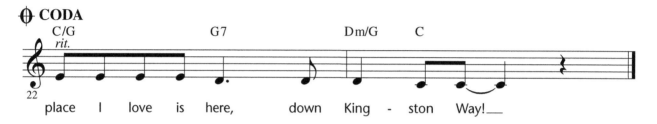

C/G   G7   Dm/G   C
rit.

place   I   love   is   here,   down   King - ston   Way!___

Latin

La bamba

Audio Access

BOOMWHACKERS – Notes Used: C, E, F, G, A, B

Traditional
Arranged by TOM ANDERSON

The original purchaser of this book has permission to reproduce this song for classroom use in one school only. Any other use is strictly prohibited.

BoomWhack Attack!

Latin

La bamba

VOCALS

PERCUSSION

Traditional
Arranged by TOM ANDERSON

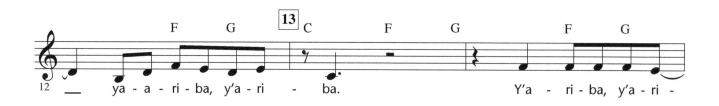

Copyright © 2005 by HAL LEONARD CORPORATION
International Copyright Secured   All Rights Reserved

BoomWhack Attack!

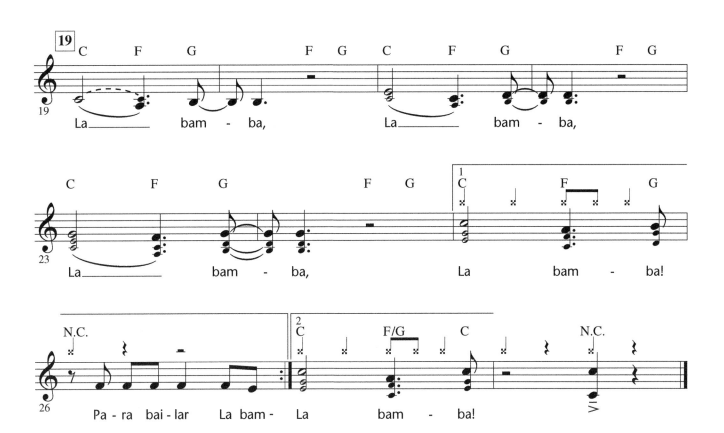

BoomWhack Attack!

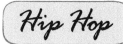

Mama Don't 'Low

Audio Access

American
Arranged by TOM ANDERSON

BoomWhack Attack!

Hip Hop

Mama Don't 'Low

VOCALS

American
Arranged by TOM ANDERSON

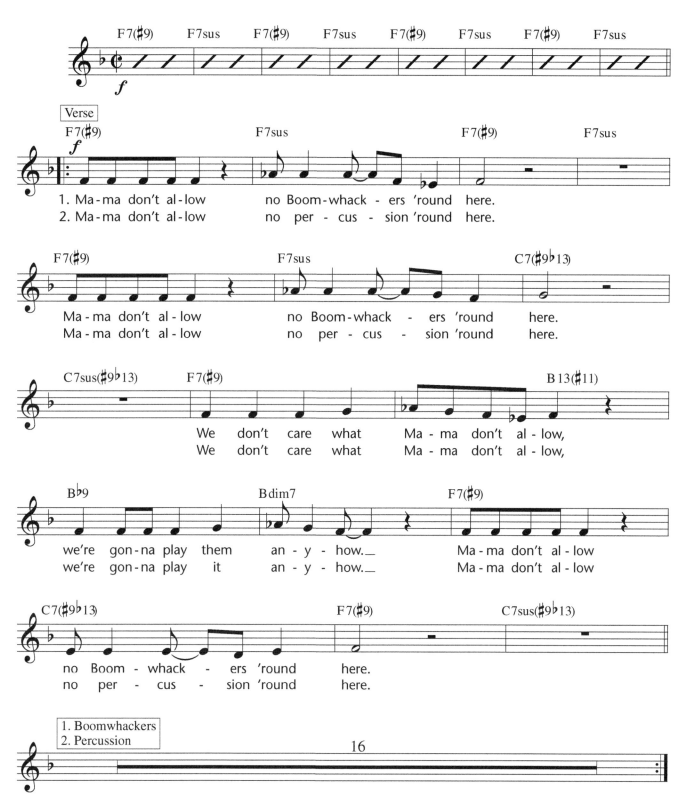

BoomWhack Attack!

Rap Section

Rhythm, rhyme and poetry; comes to us so nat'rally.
East coast, west coast; all around. Listen to our funky sound.
Come on, Mama, join the fun. We're her daughters. We're the sons.
That's more like it: Mama's cool. Now she's breakin' all the rules!

D.S. al Coda
(to Verse 4)

CODA

Pomp and Circumstance

BOOMWHACKERS – Notes Used: C, D, E, F, G, A, C'

Music by EDWARD ELGAR
Arranged by TOM ANDERSON

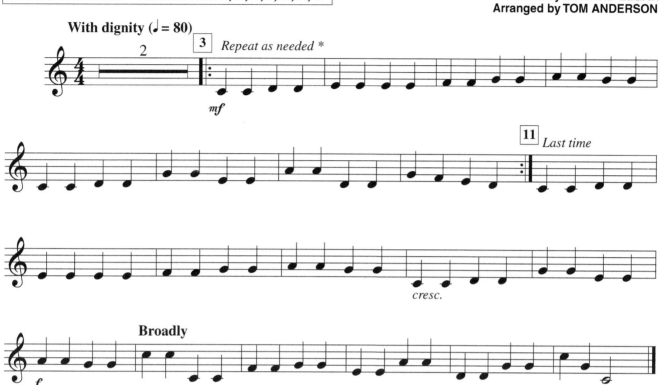

* played 3 times on recording

Here are some ideas for playing this piece at your next graduation or promotion.

- Continue repeating until all of the graduates have processed into place.
- Form a Boomwhacker® choir at the front of the gym or auditorium playing them on the floor or tapping them with your hand.
- All the Boomwhacker® players could wear graduation hats that have tassels.
- At the end of the ceremony throw your hats in the air in celebration of a job well-done.

BoomWhack Attack!

Pomp and Circumstance

PIANO

Music by EDWARD ELGAR
Arranged by TOM ANDERSON

played 3 times on recording

BoomWhack Attack!

Rig-a-Jig-Jig

19th Century Game Song
Arranged by TOM ANDERSON

BOOMWHACKERS — Notes Used: C, D, G, B, C'

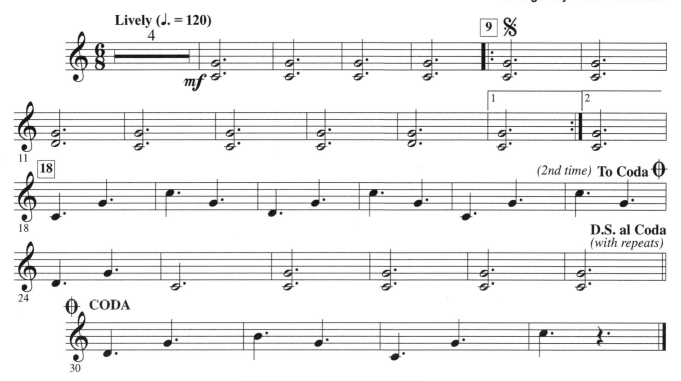

19th Century Game Song
Arranged by TOM ANDERSON

PERCUSSION

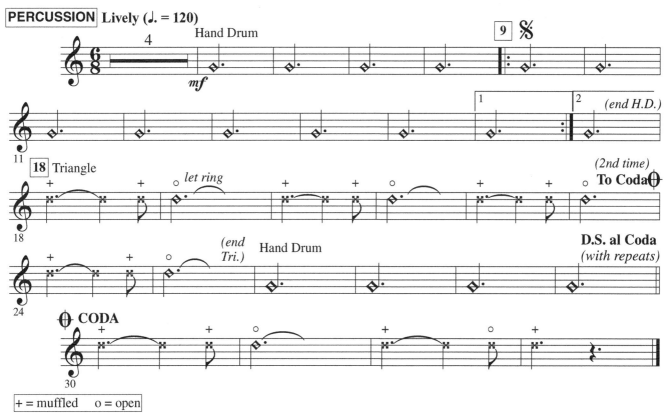

+ = muffled   o = open

BoomWhack Attack!

Rig-a-Jig-Jig

VOCALS

19th Century Game Song
Arranged by TOM ANDERSON

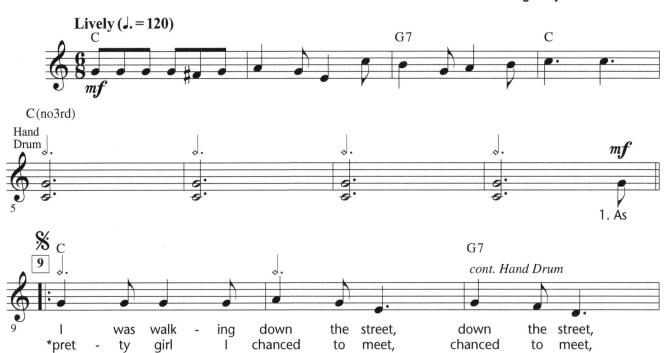

I was walk - ing down the street, down the street,
*pret - ty girl I chanced to meet, chanced to meet,

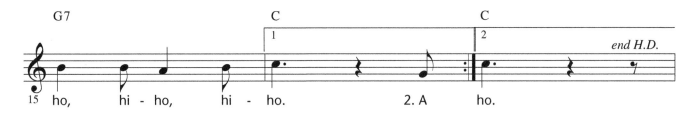

down the street, As I was walk - ing down the street, Hi -
chanced to meet, A pret - ty girl I chanced to meet, Hi -

ho, hi - ho, hi - ho. 2. A ho.

Rig - a - jig jig, and a - way we go, A - way we go, a -

* May use handsome boy

+ = muffled   o = open

BoomWhack Attack!

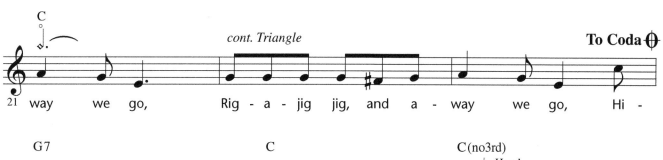

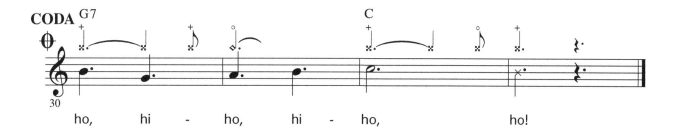

ho, hi - ho, hi - ho, ho!

Additional verses for D. S.

3. I asked her would she walk with me,
   walk with me, walk with me,
   I asked her would she walk with me,
   Hi-ho...

4. She said, "Kind sir, I'll walk with ye,
   walk with ye, walk with ye."
   She said, "Kind sir, I'll walk with ye,"
   Hi-ho...

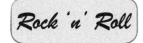

Rockin' Robin

Audio
Access

BOOMWHACKERS – Notes Used: C, F, G, B, C'

Words and Music by
J. THOMAS
Arranged by TOM ANDERSON

There is a two-measure introduction on recording.

Bright Rock Shuffle (♩ = 162)

D.S. al Coda

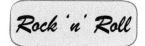

Rockin' Robin

VOCALS

Words and Music by
J. THOMAS
Arranged by TOM ANDERSON

There is a two-measure introduction on recording.

Bright Rock Shuffle (♩ = 162)

Handclaps on beats 2 and 4

(Boomwhackers)

1. He

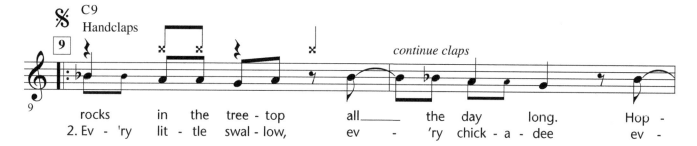

rocks in the tree-top all the day long. Hop-

2. Ev-'ry lit-tle swal-low, ev-'ry chick-a-dee ev-

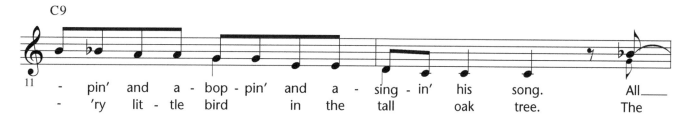

-pin' and a-bop-pin' and a-sing-in' his song. All

-'ry lit-tle bird in the tall oak tree. The

the lit-tle birds on Jay-bird street, love

wise old owl the big black crow, flap-

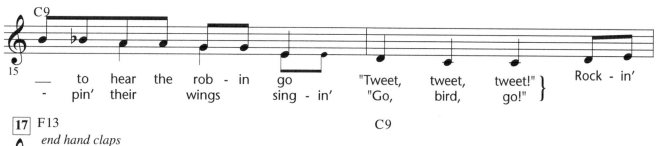

to hear the rob-in go "Tweet, tweet, tweet!" Rock-in'

-pin' their wings sing-in' "Go, bird, go!"

end hand claps

Rob-in, Rock-in' Rob-in,

BoomWhack Attack!

JAZZ

A-Tisket A-Tasket

Audio
Access

BOOMWHACKERS – Notes Used: C, D, E, F, G, A, B, C'

Traditional
Arranged by TOM ANDERSON

Copyright © 2006 by HAL LEONARD CORPORATION
International Copyright Secured   All Rights Reserved

BoomWhack Attack!

A-Tisket A-Tasket

VOCALS

Traditional
Arranged by TOM ANDERSON

BoomWhack Attack!

Up on the Housetop

BOOMWHACKERS – Notes Used: C, D, E, F, G, A, C'

Traditional
Arranged by TOM ANDERSON

Copyright © 2004 by HAL LEONARD CORPORATION
International Copyright Secured All Rights Reserved

Up on the Housetop

Audio Access

PERCUSSION

Traditional
Arranged by TOM ANDERSON

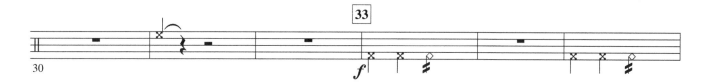

BoomWhack Attack!

Up on the Housetop

Traditional
Arranged by TOM ANDERSON

About the Arranger

Tom Anderson

Tom Anderson is a Choral Editor for Hal Leonard Corporation. A music educator for over 20 years, Tom has taught at the kindergarten through university levels in Montana, Colorado, Pennsylvania and Washington state. He holds a Master in Music Education degree from the University of North Texas and a DMA in Choral Conducting from the University of Missouri-Kansas City. His choral arrangements are published by Hal Leonard which also publishes his books such as *Music Fact Raps, Percussion Cookbook, Harmony Cookbook, Whacked on Classics,* and *Whacked on Classics II.* Tom is an active musician who plays the piano, guitar, bass and drums.

 HOW TO ACCESS DIGITAL RECORDINGS

1. To access content in Hal Leonard's MY LIBRARY, go to **www.halleonard.com/mylibrary**.

2. Follow the instructions to set up your own My Library account, so that codes are saved for future access, and you don't have to re-enter them every time.

3. Once you have created your own library account, then enter the 16-digit product code listed on page 1.

4. **Important:** Follow the instructions on the "Read Me First" PDFs for Mac and PC to **properly** download, unzip, open and use these digital files.